THIS BOC

M000013409

NAME _____

ADDRESS _____

PHONE _____

EMAIL _____

NOTES _____

_____

_____

_____

_____

_____

_____

PHONE BOOK

NAME	PHONE

PHONE BOOK

NAME	PHONE

PHONE BOOK

NAME	PHONE

PHONE BOOK

NAME	PHONE

Date _____ Speaker _____

Topic _____

Scripture References

_____

_____

Notes

Prayer Requests

Keywords

Further Study

Date _____ Speaker _____

Topic _____

Scripture References

....

....

Notes	Prayer Requests

Further Study	Keywords

Date _____   Speaker _____

Topic _____

Scripture References

_____

_____

Notes

Prayer Requests

Further Study

Keywords

Date _____   Speaker _____

Topic _____

Scripture References

....

....

Notes

Prayer Requests

Keywords

Further Study

Date _____ Speaker _____

Topic _____

Scripture References

_____

_____

Notes	Prayer Requests

Further Study

Keywords

Date _____   Speaker _____

Topic _____

Scripture References

....

....

Notes	Prayer Requests

Further Study

Keywords

Date _____ Speaker _____

Topic _____

Scripture References

_____

_____

Notes	Prayer Requests

Further Study

Keywords

Date _____ Speaker _____

Topic _____

Scripture References

....

....

Notes	Prayer Requests

Further Study

Keywords

Date _____   Speaker _____

Topic _____

Scripture References

_____

_____

Notes	Prayer Requests

Further Study

Keywords

Date _____   Speaker _____

Topic _____

Scripture References

_____
_____

Notes	Prayer Requests

Further Study

Keywords

Date _____   Speaker _____

Topic _____

Scripture References

_____

_____

Notes

Prayer Requests

Keywords

Further Study

Date _____ Speaker _____

Topic _____

Scripture References

....

....

Notes	Prayer Requests

Keywords

Further Study

Date _____   Speaker _____

Topic _____

Scripture References

_____

_____

Notes	Prayer Requests

Further Study

Keywords

Date _____   Speaker _____

Topic _____

Scripture References

....

....

Notes	Prayer Requests

Further Study

Keywords

Date _____   Speaker _____

Topic _____

Scripture References

_____

_____

Notes	Prayer Requests

Further Study

Keywords

Date _____   Speaker _____

Topic _____

Scripture References

....

....

Notes	Prayer Requests

Further Study

Keywords

Date _____   Speaker _____

Topic _____

Scripture References

_____

_____

Notes	Prayer Requests

Further Study

Keywords

Date _____ Speaker _____

Topic _____

Scripture References

....

....

Notes	Prayer Requests

Further Study

Keywords

Date _____ Speaker _____

Topic _____

Scripture References

_____

_____

Notes

Prayer Requests

Keywords

Further Study

Date _____ Speaker _____

Topic _____

Scripture References

....

....

Notes

Prayer Requests

Further Study

Keywords

Date _____   Speaker _____

Topic _____

Scripture References

_____

_____

Notes	Prayer Requests

Further Study

Keywords

Date _____ Speaker _____

Topic _____

Scripture References

....

_____

Notes	Prayer Requests

Keywords

Further Study

Date _____ Speaker _____

Topic _____

Scripture References

_____

_____

Notes	Prayer Requests

Keywords

Further Study

Date _____   Speaker _____

Topic _____

Scripture References

....

....

Notes	Prayer Requests

Further Study

Keywords

Date _____   Speaker _____

Topic _____

Scripture References

_____

_____

Notes

Prayer Requests

Keywords

Further Study

Date _____   Speaker _____

Topic _____

Scripture References

....

....

Notes

Prayer Requests

Keywords

Further Study

Date _____   Speaker _____

Topic _____

Scripture References

_____

_____

Notes	Prayer Requests

Further Study

Keywords

Date _____   Speaker _____

Topic _____

Scripture References

....

_____

Notes

Prayer Requests

Keywords

Further Study

Date _____ Speaker _____

Topic _____

Scripture References

_____

_____

Notes

Prayer Requests

Further Study

Keywords

Date _____   Speaker _____

Topic _____

Scripture References

....

_____

Notes	Prayer Requests

Further Study	Keywords

Date _____   Speaker _____

Topic _____

Scripture References

_____

_____

Notes

Prayer Requests

Keywords

Further Study

Date _____   Speaker _____

Topic _____

Scripture References

_____

_____

Notes

Prayer Requests

Keywords

Further Study

Date _____   Speaker _____

Topic _____

Scripture References

_____

_____

Notes

Prayer Requests

Keywords

Further Study

Date _____   Speaker _____

Topic _____

Scripture References

....

....

Notes

Prayer Requests

Further Study

Keywords

Date _____   Speaker _____

Topic _____

Scripture References

_____

_____

Notes	Prayer Requests

Further Study

Keywords

Date _____   Speaker _____

Topic _____

Scripture References

....

....

Notes	Prayer Requests

Further Study

Keywords

Date _____   Speaker _____

Topic _____

Scripture References

_____

_____

Notes	Prayer Requests

Keywords

Further Study

Date _____   Speaker _____

Topic _____

Scripture References

....

....

Notes	Prayer Requests

Keywords

Further Study

Date _____   Speaker _____

Topic _____

Scripture References

_____

_____

Notes

Prayer Requests

Keywords

Further Study

Date _____   Speaker _____

Topic _____

Scripture References

_____

_____

Notes	Prayer Requests

Further Study

Keywords

Date _____ Speaker _____

Topic _____

Scripture References

_____

_____

Notes	Prayer Requests

Further Study

Keywords

Date _____ Speaker _____

Topic _____

Scripture References

_____

_____

Notes	Prayer Requests

Further Study

Keywords

Date _____   Speaker _____

Topic _____

Scripture References

_____

_____

Notes

Prayer Requests

Keywords

Further Study

Date _____   Speaker _____

Topic _____

Scripture References

....

....

Notes	Prayer Requests

Further Study

Keywords

Date _____   Speaker _____

Topic _____

Scripture References

_____

_____

Notes	Prayer Requests

Further Study

Keywords

Date _____   Speaker _____

Topic _____

Scripture References

....

....

Notes	Prayer Requests

Further Study

Keywords

Date _____ Speaker _____

Topic _____

Scripture References

_____

_____

Notes

Prayer Requests

Further Study

Keywords

Date _____   Speaker _____

Topic _____

Scripture References

....

....

Notes

Prayer Requests

Further Study

Keywords

Date _____   Speaker _____

Topic _____

Scripture References

_____

_____

Notes	Prayer Requests

Further Study

Keywords

Date _____   Speaker _____

Topic _____

Scripture References

_____

_____

Notes	Prayer Requests

Further Study

Keywords

Date _____ Speaker _____

Topic _____

Scripture References

_____

_____

Notes

Prayer Requests

Further Study

Keywords

Date _____   Speaker _____

Topic _____

Scripture References

_____

_____

Notes

Prayer Requests

Keywords

Further Study

Date _____   Speaker _____

Topic _____

Scripture References

_____

_____

Notes	Prayer Requests

Further Study

Keywords

Date _____   Speaker _____

Topic _____

Scripture References

_____

_____

Notes	Prayer Requests

Further Study

Keywords

Date _____ Speaker _____

Topic _____

Scripture References

_____

_____

Notes	Prayer Requests

Further Study

Keywords

Date _____ Speaker _____

Topic _____

Scripture References

_____

_____

Notes

Prayer Requests

Keywords

Further Study

Date _____   Speaker _____

Topic _____

Scripture References

_____

_____

Notes	Prayer Requests

Further Study

Keywords

Date _____   Speaker _____

Topic _____

Scripture References

_____

_____

Notes	Prayer Requests

Further Study

Keywords

Date _____ Speaker _____

Topic _____

Scripture References

....

....

Notes	Prayer Requests

Keywords

Further Study

Date _____   Speaker _____

Topic _____

Scripture References

_____

_____

Notes	Prayer Requests

Further Study

Keywords

Date _____   Speaker _____

Topic _____

Scripture References

....

....

Notes

Prayer Requests

Further Study

Keywords

Date _____   Speaker _____

Topic _____

Scripture References

_____

_____

Notes	Prayer Requests

Further Study

Keywords

Date _____ Speaker _____

Topic _____

Scripture References

_____

_____

Notes	Prayer Requests

Keywords

Further Study

Date _____   Speaker _____

Topic _____

Scripture References

_____

_____

Notes	Prayer Requests

Further Study	Keywords

Date _____ Speaker _____

Topic _____

Scripture References

_____

_____

Notes

Prayer Requests

Keywords

Further Study

Date _____   Speaker _____

Topic _____

Scripture References

_____

_____

Notes	Prayer Requests

Further Study

Keywords

Date _____ Speaker _____

Topic _____

Scripture References

_____

_____

Notes

Prayer Requests

Keywords

Further Study

Date _____   Speaker _____

Topic _____

Scripture References

_____

_____

Notes	Prayer Requests

Keywords

Further Study

Date _____   Speaker _____

Topic _____

Scripture References

_____

_____

Notes	Prayer Requests

Further Study

Keywords

Date _____ Speaker _____

Topic _____

Scripture References

_____

_____

Notes	Prayer Requests

Further Study	Keywords

Date _____   Speaker _____

Topic _____

Scripture References

_____

_____

Notes

Prayer Requests

Keywords

Further Study

Date _____ Speaker _____

Topic _____

Scripture References

_____

_____

Notes

Prayer Requests

Keywords

Further Study

Date _____   Speaker _____

Topic _____

Scripture References

_____

_____

Notes

Prayer Requests

Keywords

Further Study

Date _____   Speaker _____

Topic _____

Scripture References

_____

_____

Notes	Prayer Requests

Further Study	Keywords

Date _____   Speaker _____

Topic _____

Scripture References

_____

_____

Notes	Prayer Requests

Further Study

Keywords

Date _____   Speaker _____

Topic _____

Scripture References

_____

_____

Notes	Prayer Requests

Further Study

Keywords

Date _____   Speaker _____

Topic _____

Scripture References

_____

_____

Notes	Prayer Requests

Further Study

Keywords

Date _____   Speaker _____

Topic _____

Scripture References

_____

_____

Notes

Prayer Requests

Further Study

Keywords

Date _____   Speaker _____

Topic _____

Scripture References

_____

_____

Notes	Prayer Requests

Further Study

Keywords

Date _____   Speaker _____

Topic _____

Scripture References

_____

_____

Notes	Prayer Requests

Further Study

Keywords

Date _____ Speaker _____

Topic _____

Scripture References

_____

_____

Notes	Prayer Requests

Further Study	Keywords

Date _____   Speaker _____

Topic _____

Scripture References

_____

_____

Notes	Prayer Requests

Further Study

Keywords

Date _____   Speaker _____

Topic _____

Scripture References

....

....

Notes	Prayer Requests

Further Study

Keywords

Date _____   Speaker _____

Topic _____

Scripture References

_____

_____

Notes	Prayer Requests

Further Study

	Keywords

Date _____ Speaker _____

Topic _____

Scripture References

_____

_____

Notes	Prayer Requests

Further Study	Keywords

Date _____   Speaker _____

Topic _____

Scripture References

_____

_____

Notes	Prayer Requests

Further Study

Keywords

Date _____   Speaker _____

Topic _____

Scripture References

_____

_____

Notes

Prayer Requests

Keywords

Further Study

Date _____   Speaker _____

Topic _____

Scripture References

_____

_____

Notes	Prayer Requests

Further Study

Keywords

Date _____   Speaker _____

Topic _____

Scripture References

_____

_____

Notes	Prayer Requests

Further Study

Keywords

Date _____   Speaker _____

Topic _____

Scripture References

_____

_____

Notes	Prayer Requests

Further Study	Keywords

Date _____   Speaker _____

Topic _____

Scripture References

_____

_____

Notes

Prayer Requests

Further Study

Keywords

Date _____   Speaker _____

Topic _____

Scripture References

_____

_____

Notes	Prayer Requests

Further Study	Keywords

Date _____ Speaker _____

Topic _____

Scripture References

_____

_____

Notes	Prayer Requests

Keywords

Further Study

Date _____   Speaker _____

Topic _____

Scripture References

_____

_____

Notes	Prayer Requests

Further Study

Keywords

Date _____   Speaker _____

Topic _____

Scripture References

_____

_____

Notes

Prayer Requests

Further Study

Keywords

Date _____   Speaker _____

Topic _____

Scripture References

_____

_____

Notes

Prayer Requests

Keywords

Further Study

Date _____   Speaker _____

Topic _____

Scripture References

_____

_____

Notes

Prayer Requests

Keywords

Further Study

Date _____ Speaker _____

Topic _____

Scripture References

_____

_____

Notes	Prayer Requests

Further Study

Keywords

Date _____ Speaker _____

Topic _____

Scripture References

_____

_____

Notes	Prayer Requests

Further Study

Keywords

Date _____   Speaker _____

Topic _____

Scripture References

_____

_____

Notes	Prayer Requests

Keywords

Further Study

Date _____   Speaker _____

Topic _____

Scripture References

_____

_____

Notes

Prayer Requests

Keywords

Further Study

Date _____ Speaker _____

Topic _____

Scripture References

_____

_____

Notes	Prayer Requests

Further Study	Keywords

Made in the USA
Middletown, DE
17 January 2022